# FARYMANN MARINE DIESEL ENGINE

*Service Manual*

**FARYMANN MARINE DIESEL ENGINE**

Service Manual

ISBN/EAN: 9783954272372
Erscheinungsjahr: 2012
Erscheinungsort: Bremen, Deutschland

© maritimepress in Europäischer Hochschulverlag GmbH & Co. KG, Fahrenheitstr. 1, 28359 Bremen. Alle Rechte beim Verlag und bei den jeweiligen Lizenzgebern.

www.maritimepress.de | office@maritimepress.de

Bei diesem Titel handelt es sich um den Nachdruck eines historischen, lange vergriffenen Buches. Da elektronische Druckvorlagen für diese Titel nicht existieren, musste auf alte Vorlagen zurückgegriffen werden. Hieraus zwangsläufig resultierende Qualitätsverluste bitten wir zu entschuldigen.

# FARYMANN MARINE DIESEL ENGINE

*Service Manual*

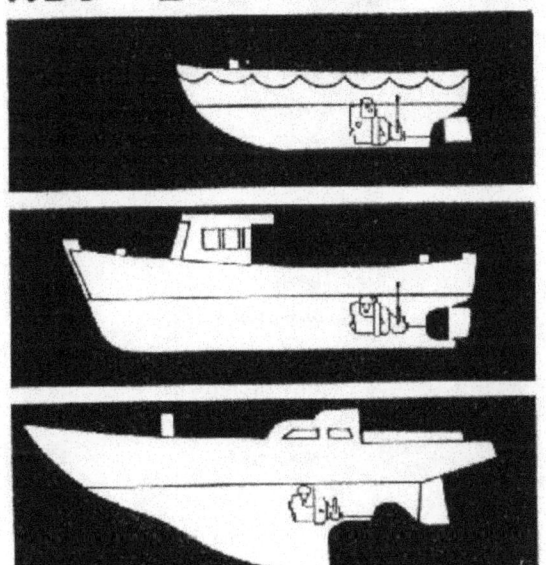

## CONTENTS

| | |
|---|---|
| Technical data | 3 |
| Description of engines | 4 |
| Description of gearbox | 8 |
| Preparation for initial start-up | 8 |
|     Marking on oil dipstick | 0 |
|     Fuel and lub.-oil | 11 |
| Daily checks | 12 |
| Starting up the engine | 13 |
|     Hand starting | 13 |
|     Electric starting | 14 |
|     Stopping | 15 |
| Frost hazard | 15 |
| Care and maintenance | 16 |
|     Time schedule | 16 |
|     Engine | 16 |
|     Gearbox | 16 |
| Storage of engine | 22 |
|     Electric system | 23 |
| Restoring to service | 23 |
| Trouble shooting | 24 |
| Technical information sheets | |
|     Fuel system | 27 |
|     Cooling water circuit | 28 |
|     Electrical wiring diagrams | 30 |
|     Remote control | 33 |

**Farymann Diesel**

## TECHNICAL DATA

| ENGINE | K 30 | L 30 | A 30/A 40 | R 30 | P 30 | S 30 |
|---|---|---|---|---|---|---|
| Power HP | 5 | 8 | 10 | 20 | 22 | 26 |
| Speed RPM | 2500 | 2500 | 2500 | 2500 | 2500 | 2500 |
| Torque Nm | 1,5 | 2,2 | 2,9 | 5,2 | 6,3 | 7,4 |
| No. of Cyl. | 1 | 1 | 1 | 2 | 2 | 2 |
| Cubic cm | 298 | 412 | 582 | 1182 | 1276 | 1558 |

| | | | | | | |
|---|---|---|---|---|---|---|
| Valve clearance (Intake + Exh.) (cold) | | | 0.1 mm (0.004") | | | |
| Decompression device-cold | | | 1 mm (0.04") max. stroke | | | |
| Engine oil<br>  Summer<br>  Winter | | | HD SAE 20 (30)<br>HD SAE 10 (20) | | | |
| Oil filter<br>Fuel filter element | — | — | PUROLATOR PM 456 | | PUROLATOR PC 27 | |
| Reverse gear | K 34<br>FG 4 | L 30<br>FG 4 | | R 30<br>Hurth<br>HBW 5 | | S 30<br>Hurth<br>HBW 10 |
| Propeller rotation | | | right hand | | | |
| Electrical equipment<br>Min. size battery | 12 V<br>56 Ah | 56 Ah | | 88 Ah | | 88 Ah |

## DESCRIPTION OF ENGINES

K 34 M — Single cylinder, four cycle diesel engine. Direct injection. Direct sea-water cooling. Forged crankshaft with roller bearings on flywheel side. Pressure lubrication. Watercooled exhaust.

Engine K 34 M

L 30 M — Single cylinder, four cycle diesel engine. Direct injection. Direct sea-water cooling. Forged crankshaft with roller bearings for connecting rod bearings and main bearings. Splash lubrication. Watercooled exhaust.

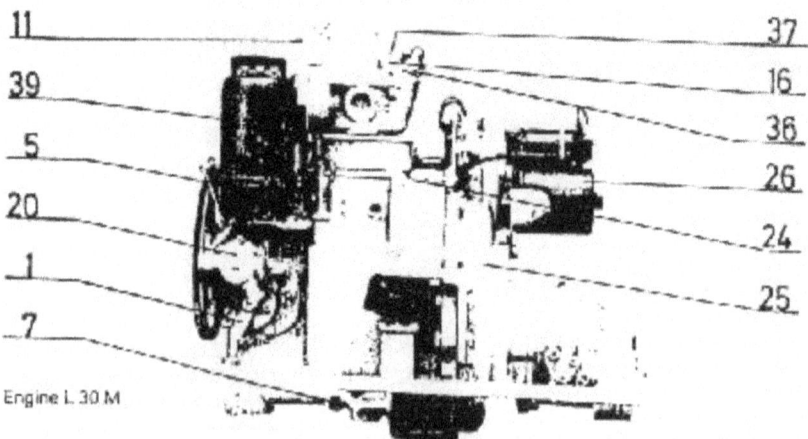

Engine L 30 M

L 30 M

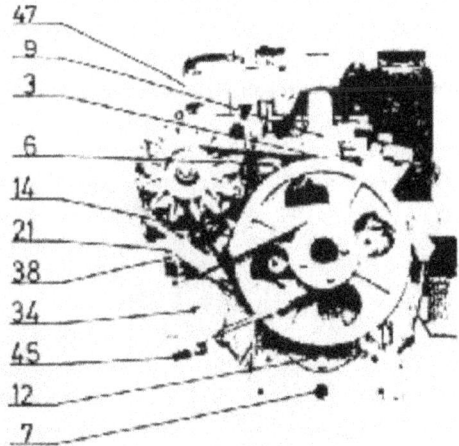

## SINGLE CYLINDER ENGINES

K 34 M vertical, L 30 M vertical

1 – Throttle control + stop lever
3 – Decompression device
5 – Oil dipstick
6 – Lube-oil filler
7 – Lube-oil drain plug
9 – Breather (crankcase)
11 – Rocker arm cover
12 – governor inspection cover
14 – Injection pump
16 – Nozzle holder
17 – Fuel return line
20 – Fuel feed pump
21 – Fuel filter
24 – Mark for TDC (remove protective cover)
25 – Flywheel housing flange
26 – Electric starter motor
33 – Marine mounts
34 – Water pump
36 – Thermostat
37 – Connector for thermometer
38 – Water drain
39 – Air intake silencer
40 – Oil dipstick (gearbox)
42 – Gearshift lever
43 – Connector for remote control
45 – Water inlet
47 – Elbow for water injection

A 30 M / A 40 M
K 30 M

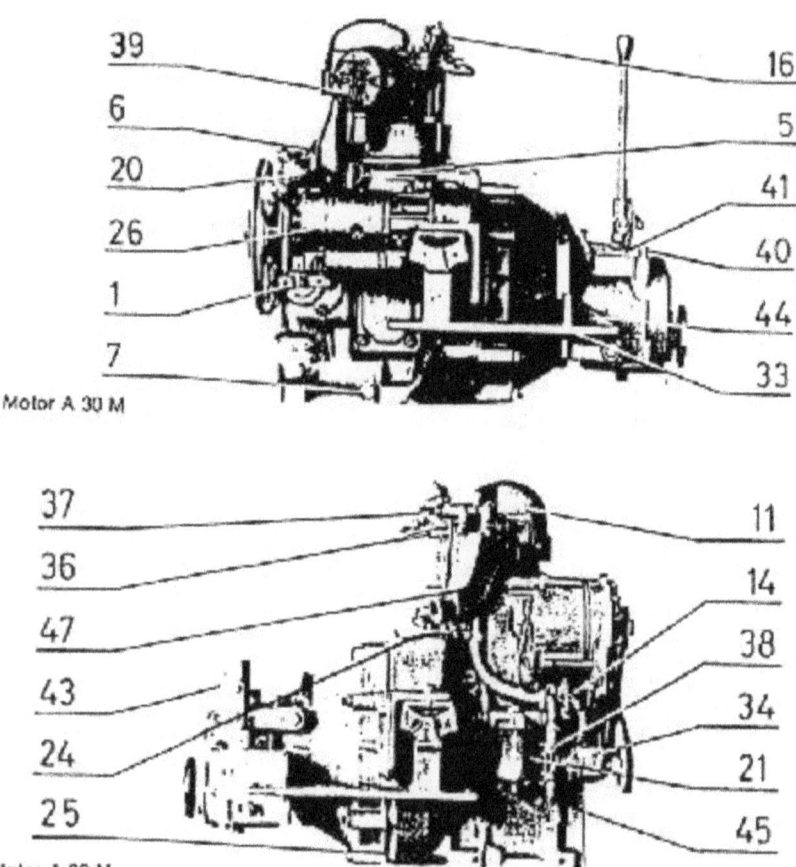

Motor A 30 M

Motor A 30 M

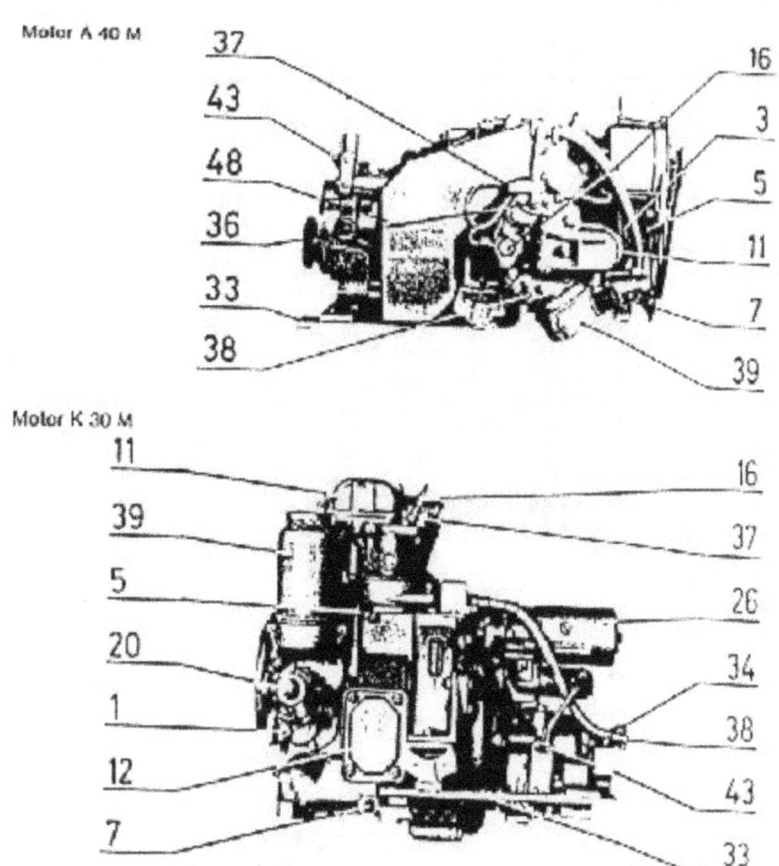

## DESCRIPTION OF ENGINES

R 30 M  
S 30 M

V-2, four-cycle diesel engines. Direct injection. Direct seawater cooled. Forged crankshaft. Roller bearings on flywheel side. Pressure lubrication. Watercooled exhaust.

Engine R 30 M

Engine S 30 M / P 30

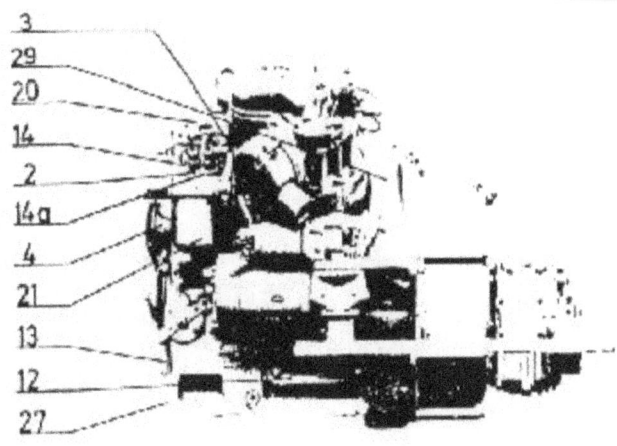

Engine S 30 M / P30

## V-2 ENGINES

R 30 M / S 30 M

1 — Speed control + stop lever
2 — Excess starting fuel
3 — Decompression device
4 — Camshaft
5 — Oil dipstick
6 — Lube-oil filler
7 — Lube-oil drain plug
9 — Breather (crankcase)
11 — Rocker arm cover
12 — Crankcase cover
13 — Governor inspection cover
14 — Injection pump
14a — Vent screw
15 — Fuel pressure line
16 — Nozzle holder
17 — Fuel return line
20 — Fuel feed pump
21 — Fuel filter
25 — Flywheel housing flange

26 — Electric starter motor
27 — Oil strainer
28 — Crankcase cover
29 — Inspection cover
30 — Lube-oil filter
31 — Oil cooler
32 — Oil pressure switch
33 — Marine mounts
34 — Water pump
36 — Thermostat
37 — Connector for thermometer
38 — Water drain
39 — Air intake silencer
40 — Oil dipstick (gearbox)
42 — Gearshift lever
43 — Connector for remote control
45 — Water inlet
46 — Water outlet

## MARINE REVERSE REDUCTION GEARBOX

| Engine Type | K 30 M | L 30 M | A 30 M/A 40 M | R 30 M | P 30 M | S 30 M |
|---|---|---|---|---|---|---|
| Manufacturer | Ronim | | | Hurth | Hurth | Hurth |
| Type | Ro | FG 3 | FG 3 | HBW 10 | HBW 10 | HBW 10 |

### FG 4-Gearbox

Gearbox is fitted with 2 cone clutches and respective servo-engaging mechanism. Oil check through insert-type dipstick.

For spare parts ordering please always state engine number and engine type, which have been marked on the gear housing.

### HURTH-Gearbox

Hurth marine gearboxes are helical gear transmissions shifted via 2 internal mechanical friction clutches, designed to permit reversing operations at full engine speed in case of emergency. As clutches are exactly set as to nominal torque, shock loads from propeller or shaft will not be transmitted to gearbox or engine.

Oil check by threaded dipstick. When checking oil, just insert dipstick – do not thread in. After check put in and retighten.

For spare parts ordering please always state engine number and engine type, which have been marked on the gear housing.

## 1. PREPARATION FOR INITIAL START-UP

1.1  Check bolt and hose connecting and all pipework for leaks and tighten nuts and bolts if necessary. This applies especially to the mounting bolts and the retaining bolts on the exhaust and shaft assembly.

1.2  Mark oil dipstick of engine according to the inclination of the engine in the fully loaded boat.

1.3  Fill tank with fuel.

Engine and gears are not filled with oil by suppliers. Make sure that both oil drain plugs are tight.

**IMPORTANT**: absolute cleanliness is essential when filling up. The area around the filler should be cleaned before opening it. Use only clean containers, funnels or strainers.

## LUBRICATING OIL:

Use only well known HD brands of engine oil, and keep to the brand selected, if at all possible. Never mix different brands when topping up the oil.

|         | Summer        | Winter        |
|---------|---------------|---------------|
| Engine  | HD SAE 20 (30)| HD SAE 10 (20)|
| Gearbox | HD SAE 30     | HD SAE 30     |

The engine oil can also be used for lubricating the gearbox but not vice versa. Hurth gearbox uses automatic transmission fluid type A.

**Attention:** for engines HD oils should be used only.

**WARNING:** Additives such as molybdenum sulphate or the like must not be contained in the gearbox oil under any circumstances.

## CORRECTION OF DIPSTICK – ENGINE UNDER INCLINATION

Usual installation: Flywheel side (gearbox) lower than engine itself.

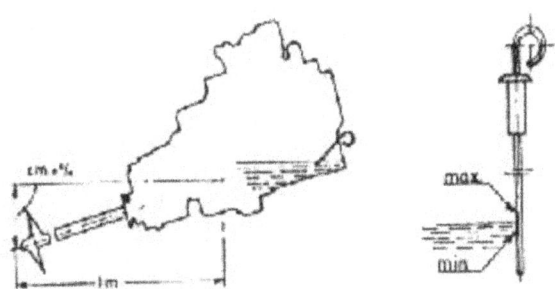

Markings on dipstick for horizontal installation (if any) have to be removed and re-adjusted in accordance with the engine slope. After complete installation of engine into boat fill up the exact quantity of lube-oil according to the slope and engine type (see chart on page 10). Thus determined oil level should be marked on the dipstick with an auxiliary mark. 5 mm above and 10 mm below the definite marks for "max" respectively "min" level should be filed in.

**CAUTION:** Given oil quantities must not be exceeded. Overfilling results in overheating and destruction.

| Inclination | Degree | 0° – 10° | | 11° – 15° | |
| --- | --- | --- | --- | --- | --- |
| | Percent | 0% – 18% | | 19% – 26% | |
| | cm | 0 – 18 | | 19 – 26 | |
| Lube-oil quantity in crankshaft housing ltr/US pints | | ltr. | US pints | ltr. | US pints |
| | K 34 M | 1.0 | 2.2 | 0.9 | 1.9 |
| | L 30 M | 1.4 | 3.0 | 1.0 | 2.1 |
| | S 30 M | 3.3 | 7.0 | 3.0 | 6.3 |

R 30 M   *R 30  2,0*

Standard spec. includes rod dipstick. If the actual engine inclination does not correspond to char below, respective dipstick has to be ordered.

| Inclination | Degree | 0° – 6° | | 6° – 12° | | 12° – 15° | |
| --- | --- | --- | --- | --- | --- | --- | --- |
| | Percent | 0% – 11% | | 11% – 21% | | 21% – 26% | |
| | cm | 0 – 11 | | 11 – 21 | | 21 – 26 | |
| Lube-oil quantity in crankshaft housing | | ltr. | US pint | ltr. | US pint | ltr. | US pint |
| | | 3.0 | 6.3 | 2.8 | 5.9 | 2.5 | 5.3 |
| Dipstick colour code | | black | | red | | green | |

Oil quantities stated for 2-cylinder engines are only valid, if oil filter has not been replaced. When replacing oil-filter, an additional 0,3 l oil has to be filled in.

## REVERSE GEAR OIL CAPACITY

| | GEARBOX | | | |
| --- | --- | --- | --- | --- |
| | Liter | | US. quart | |
| TYP | Ronim Nanni | Hurth | Ronim Nanni | Hurth |
| | FG 3 | | FG 3 | |

| Inclination | Degree | 0° – 10° | | 11° – 15° | |
|---|---|---|---|---|---|
| | Percent | 0% – 18% | | 19% – 26% | |
| | cm | 0 – 18 | | 19 – 26 | |
| Lube-oil quantity in crankshaft housing ltr/US pints | | ltr. | US pints | ltr. | US pints |
| | K 34 M | 1.0 | 2.2 | 0.9 | 1.9 |
| | L 30 M | 1.4 | 3.0 | 1.0 | 2.1 |
| | S 30 M | 3.3 | 7.0 | 3.0 | 6.3 |

R 30 M     A 30     2,0

Standard spec. includes red dipstick. If the actual engine inclination does not correspond to chart below, respective dipstick has to be ordered.

| Inclination | Degree | 0° – 6° | | 6° – 12° | | 12° – 15° | |
|---|---|---|---|---|---|---|---|
| | Percent | 0% – 11% | | 11% – 21% | | 21% – 26% | |
| | cm | 0 – 11 | | 11 – 21 | | 21 – 26 | |
| Lube-oil quantity in crankshaft housing | | ltr. | US pint | ltr. | US pint | ltr. | US pint |
| | | 3.0 | 6.3 | 2.8 | 5.9 | 2.5 | 5.3 |
| Dipstick colour code | | black | | red | | green | |

Oil quantities stated for 2-cylinder engines are only valid, if oil filter has not been replaced. When replacing oil filter, an additional 0,3 l oil has to be filled in.

## REVERSE GEAR OIL CAPACITY

| | GEARBOX | | | | | | |
|---|---|---|---|---|---|---|---|
| | Liter | | | | US. quart | | |
| TYP | Ronim Nanni | FG 3 | Hurth | | Ronim Nanni | FG 3 | Hurth |
| K 30 M | 0,3 | 0,4 | | | 0,32 | 0,44 | |
| L 30 M | | 0,4 | | | | 0,44 | |
| A 30 M | 0,6 | 0,4 | | | 0,64 | 0,44 | |
| A 40 M | 0,6 | 0,4 | | | 0,64 | 0,44 | |
| R 30 M | 0,6 | | 0,54 | | 0,64 | | 0,57 |
| P 30 M | 0,6 | | 0,54 | | 0,64 | | 0,57 |
| S 30 M | 1,0 | | 0,54 | | 1,10 | | 0,57 |

## RECOMMENDED HD-ENGINE LUBE-OILS

(Other brands of HD Lube-oils of same quality not mentioned below can equally be used.)

| Company | HD-LUBE-OILS according to API Classification | |
|---|---|---|
| | CC | CD |
| AGIP | Agip F. 1 Diesel Gamma | Agip F. 1 Diesel Sigma |
| ARAL | Aral Kowal Engine Oil<br>Aral oils of the HD-range | Aral Kowal S 3 Engine Oil<br>Aral oil HD S 3 |
| BAYWA | BayWa Engine oil HD-super<br>BayWa engine oil HD-B | BayWa HD Superior S 3<br>BayWa Universal HD |
| BP | BP Energol HD<br>BP Energol DS-B<br>BP Vanellus/Vanellus-T | BP Vanellus S 3<br>BP Energol DS 3 |
| CHEVRON | Chevron Delo Special Oil<br>Chevron Delo 200 Engine Oil | Chevron Delo 300 Engine Oil |
| ELF | elf Performance | elf Disel HD 3 |
| ESSO | Essolube HDX<br>Essolube SDX | Essolube D-3<br>Esso Estor D-3 |
| FINA | Fina Solna HD S 1<br>Fina Delta Engine Oil | Fina Sona S 6 |
| FUCHS | Renolin HD<br>Pena Pura HD<br>Pena Pura HD Super<br>Pena Pura Universal HD | Pena Pura HD Superior<br>Pena Pura Universal HD |
| MOBIL | Mobil Delvac 1100<br>Mobil Delvac 1200 | Mobil Delvac 1200<br>Mobil Delvac 1300 |
| SHELL | Shell Rotella SX/Rotella TX<br>Shell Melina Oils<br>Shell Talona Oils | Shell Rimula CT |
| TOTAL | Total HD 1 B<br>Total HP D | Total HD 3<br>Total HP D |

Working conditions, oil change interval and API classification (oil quality):

| Condition | Working Hours | API Classification | (Previous Designation) |
|---|---|---|---|
| Normal | 50 – 60 | CC | HD-SI or MIL-L 2104 A |
| Heavy* | 100 – 120 | CD | HD-B or MIL-L 2104 B |
| | 50 – 60 | CD | as well as MIL-L 2104 A<br>SUPPLEMENT 1 |

*  **Heavy working conditions**: Long idling periods, high ambient temperatures (above + 30°C = + 86° F) dusty environment, diesel fuel with more than 0,5 % sulphur.

b) **FUEL:**

Obtain fuel only from filling stations equipped with a pump and built-in filtering system otherwise filter the fuel yourself with a fine strainer (if necessary using a nylon stocking). Always replace the filler cap immediately.

Use clean commercial grade branded diesel fuel according to

DIN 51601 (German Standards), equivalent to
B.S. 2869: 1957 Class A (British Standards) or
A.S. No. 2 (American Standards).

The sulphur content must not exceed 0.5% (weight). A lower value is specially important for sea water-cooled engines operating at relatively low temperatures. Never use gasoline diesel fuel mixture or "Marine diesel Fuel" (heavy fuel for large engines).

**CAUTION:** Bleed the fuel system after the first filling. Never allow the tank to drain completely.

1.4. **RUNNING-IN**

A new or reconditioned engine must be carefully run in. During the first 20 hours only use full engine power for very short periods. After first 20 hours engine power can gradually be increased. A first oil change is necessary after 20 hours. Check cylinder head bolts at the same time. Retighten, when engine is cold. Tightening torques see technical data sheet.

**Attn.:** If the engine is only being used for manoeuvering in harbours, the most favourable operating temperature is never obtained due to the short time of operation. Thus it is absolutely necessary that such engines are being run one complete hour under full load and at full speed at intervals of 4 - 5 hours of operation, so that for example the valve covers on the cylinder head are heated up to approximately 60 – 70°C.

2. **DAILY CHECKS BEFORE STARTING**

2.1. Check oil level in engine and reverse gearbox. If necessary fill to the top mark on the dipstick.

The chromium-plate piston rings may cause a slightly higher lub.-oil consumption during the running-in period (80 -100 hours).

2.2. Check the diesel oil supply in tank and open the tank cock. If the engine has not been in operation for some time, the fuel system should be bled in accordance with the operating instructions.

2.3. After checking the drain cocks and the sea water filter, open the sea cock, completely, and check flow of sea water through transparent cover of sea water filter.

## 3 STARTING UP ENGINE

3.1 Move gear lever to neutral position (mid-position vertical).

3.2 Move the engine speed control lever to the full power position (max.) (A) (Fig. 1)

With Farymann Unicontrol (single lever) pull hub assembly outwards and lever into max. speed position. Thus rev. red. gears remain in idling position. (With Morse single lever control pull knob).

With the "Teknoflex" type single lever remote controls, which Farymann now generally employs, the red button has to be pushed in and lever has to be put in full load position.

Fig. 1

When using the "Morse" type two lever remote controls, the gear lever must be put into neutral position and the speed regulating lever on full load.

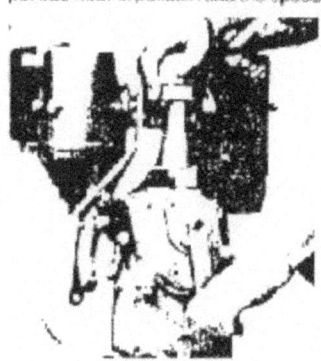

Fig. 2

Fig. 3

### 3.2.1 HAND STARTING

1) Operate lever in pushbutton (B) for starting fuel (Fig. 1)

2) Operate the decompression lever (C) (not applicable for K 34 M as this engine is fitted with automatic decompression device – for operation see K 34 manual) with your right hand and slowly turn the starting crank in the camshaft anticlockwise with your left hand. Listen for characteristic creaking of the injection nozzles.

3) Turn the crank with your left hand as fast as possible. When the maximum impetus is reached, release the decompression lever and carry on turning in order to overcome the initial compression resistance. Rapid turning, not force, is what matters!

### 3.2.2. ELECTRIC STARTING

1) Switch on electric system: Push down black button. Then pilot lamps for battery charging and oil pressure must light up. (Except engine L 30 M – Splash lubrication)

2) Push down green button and hold it there until first firing stroke. Then IMMEDIATELY let off.

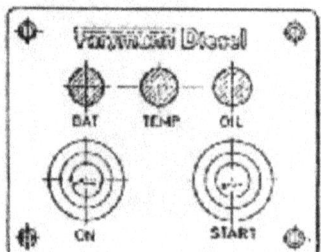
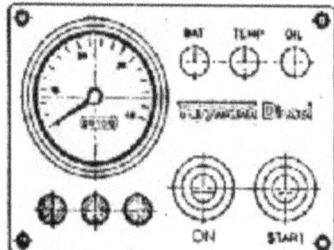

**Attention:** Limit each starting trial to 10 seconds maximum and wait for 30 – 60 seconds before repeating (to save battery). Operate starter only after engine came to a complete stop.

After engine has started and control lamps are out, run engine at medium speed under light load for warm up.

### 3.2.3. CHECKING AFTER STARTING

For most the applications, the entire cooling water is injected into the exhaust to cool down the exhaust gases (i.e. reduce the noise level), and to be able to dispose of the exhaust gases by means of rubber hose. CHECK WHETHER A FINE SPRINKLE OF WATER COMES OUT OF THE EXHAUST AND WHETHER NOISE OF EXHAUST IS NORMAL.

If no water comes out, then the exhaust produces a considerable noise which means that no cooling water is being injected into the exhaust and that cooling water supply on the engine is not in order. In this case engine has to be stopped immediately for checking.

## 3.3 STOPPING

**3.3.1** NEVER STOP THE ENGINE BY OPERATING THE DECOMPRESSION LEVER! SWITCH-OFF ELECTRIC SYSTEM ONLY AFTER ENGINE HAS COME TO A COMPLETE STOP! (Pull down black button).

**3.3.2** Never completely stop the engine while it is running at speed, but let it idle for a short time.

### SINGLE LEVER OPERATION

Farymann Unicontrol – put lever into neutral/idling position and tilt hub pulling lever outwards. Hold until engine comes to complete stop. (With Morse: pull additional stop cable and hold until engine comes to complete stop)

### TWIN LEVER OPERATION

Move the speed control lever beyond the idling position and hold it there until the engine stops.

In either case return the speed control lever to full load position as soon as the engine has stopped.

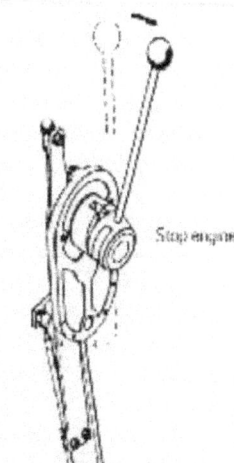

Stop engine

**3.3.3** **ELECTRICAL SYSTEM**
After stopping the engine as described above, push down black button, pilot lights expire.

**3.3.4** Close the SAE COCK (do not forget to re-open before next engine start up).

**3.3.5** Fill fuel tank after completing a run. Partially filled tank will collect moisture if engine is not operated for any length of time.

**3.3.6** **FROST HAZARD**
Open all drain cocks and ensure complete drainage. Push a wire through the cocks to ensure unimpeded flow. Finally crank the engine by hand until the cooling water pump is empty, too.

In exceptional cases, where lines or water chambers are located below the drain cocks, the appropriate pipe or hose connections must be opened in order to drain them.

Remove intake line with sea water filter from the cock!

If cooling water is injected into the engine exhaust pipe, the water lift silencer must be drained.

**3.3.7** **BATTERY**
When charged, the battery can safely withstand temperatures as low as –15° C (+ 5° F). At lower temperatures it should be removed and stored in a frost-proof place.

**ATTENTION:**
Engines equipped with A.C. generators may not be run with battery disconnected (destruction of diodes of voltage regulator). Even extremely short trial runs only with battery properly connected.

## 4. CARE AND MAINTENANCE

The operations listed in the following schedule must be repeated until the engine is due for overhaul.

### 4.1 OPERATION

| | | hours of operation | | | |
|---|---|---|---|---|---|
| ENGINE | Daily | 60 | 120 | 250 | 900 |
| Check oil level | ● | | | | |
| Change lube-oil | | | ● | | |
| Replace spin-on oil filter | | | | ● | |
| Clean oil strainer | | | | ● | |
| Flush out crankcase | | | | | ● |
| Examine nuts and bolts for tightness | | | | ● | |
| Check valve clearance | | | ● | | |
| Check sea water filter | ● | | | | |
| Check V-belt tension | ● | | | | |
| Check water pump impeller | | | ● | | |
| Examine and clean thermostat | | | | ● | |
| Check all pipelines for leaks | | ● | | | |
| Check fuel filters | | | | | ● |
| Drain (clean) fuel tank | | | ● | | |
| **GEARBOX** | | | | | |
| Change lube-oil | | | | ● | |
| Lubricate remote control mechanism | | | | ● | |
| **ELECTRICAL SYSTEM** | | | | | |
| Maintain electrolyte level in battery | ● | | | | |
| Check specific gravity of battery | | | ● | | |
| Check all cables and connections | | | ● | | |
| Grease starter ring-gear on flywheel | | | | | ● |

4.2  **CHANGE THE ENGINE OIL**

Change the oil only with the engine at operating temperature (scavenging effect), in a new engine after appr. 20 h. Change the oil again after approx. 50 – 60 hours. Later on every 120 hours.

A separate hand drain pump with hose and cock is supplied with the FAHRYMANN MARINE ENGINE.

Engine oil must be changed whenever engine is to be put out of service for extended periods.

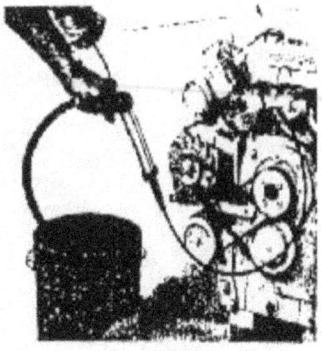

Fig. 5

4.3  **OIL FILTER**

Applies to V-2 engines.

The spin-on oil filter (1) cannot be cleaned and must be replaced.

Lightly oil the rubber seal, tighten it and top up oil level.

A suitable special spanner (2) is supplied within the tool kit.

Check for leaks with the engine running.

Filter: PUROLATOR

Type:  PC 27 (Standard)
       31 (Oversize)

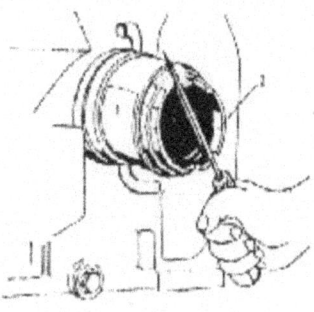

Fig. 6

4.4  **CRANKCASE**

Applies to 2-cyl. engines.

If during a normal oil change or when cleaning the oil strainer the oil is seen to contain a lot of sludge, the crankcase should be washed out sooner than recommended in the schedule. Flush with diesel oil after removing the crankcase cover.

Absolute cleanliness is essential!

Fig. 7

### 4.4. OIL STRAINING TUBE (K 34 M)

Remove oil straining tube every 500 hours and then wash out engine (with diesel fuel but not with gasoline) and clean oil sump and oil strainer as much as possible. Before reassembly again wash out with engine oil.

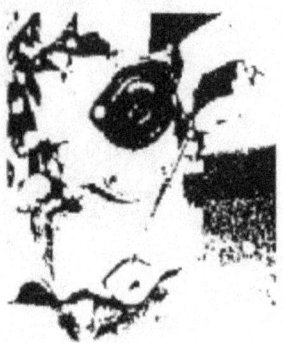

Fig. 8

Fig. 9

### 4.5. CRANKCASE BREATHER

Crankcase breather combined with oil filler should work audibly. Check with the engine running at low speed. The thin steel valve must always be kept clean. It must lie flush on its seat, otherwise it should be replaced. If necessary, take off complete breather housing and wash out thoroughly with gasoline or diesel fuel.

If there are any oil leaks on the engine, check this breather valve first.

Fig. 10

### 4.6. VALVE CLEARANCE

Adjustment on cold engine with both valves closed (TDC of firing stroke). Clearance 0.1 mm (0.004"). With new engine, valve clearance has to be checked after 20 first operating hours.

Important: after major repairs the cylinder head and rocker arm support must be firmly bolted in position with nuts to final torque tightened before valve clearance is adjusted.

Fig. 11

4.7. **V-BELT TENSION**

Too tight a belt is destructive to bearings of the driven parts. Adjust for 3/8" slack from a straight line over outer diameter of drive and driven pulleys, midway between pulleys.

4.8. **WATER PUMP IMPELLER**

The neoprene impeller has a relatively short life and must therefore be inspected regularly. If the water pump is allowed to run dry for more than a few seconds (sea cock closed) the impeller may be completely ruined. Remove cover of pump and release the impeller (c) from the shaft by applying 2 screwdrivers (E) under the hub of the impeller. Remove all traces of rubber and smooth any damaged surfaces. Fit a new impeller. A spare impeller should always be kept on board.

If impeller is held by lock screw, loosen same with screw driver thru opening (A) or remove complete shaft-impeller assembly after removing V-belt pulley.

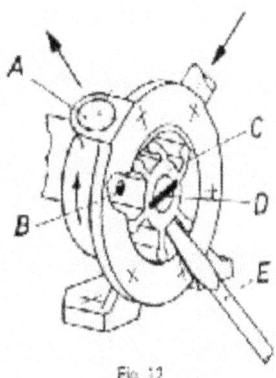

Fig. 12

4.9. **THERMOSTAT**

Farymann Diesel engines are cooled directly by sea water. The raw water never touches the engine block, but circulates only around the replaceable cylinder liner, head and exhaust system. Cooling water jacket around cylinder is constructed of a non-corrosive, glass-fibre-reinforced-plastic. Outer wall of cylinder is zincplated.

In addition, the Farymann diesel has been built to operate at cooling water temperatures below that, at which salts and minerals precipitate in sea water.

No separate fresh water cooling system is needed or recommended.

A thermostat with a setting of 55° C (120° F) is fitted to the engine. Any deposits that appear on the thermostat can be removed with dilute hydrochloric acid. Flush afterwards with fresh water.

Caution: during assembly make sure that the small hole (equipped with a tiny cotter pin) in the fitting plate of the thermostat, which permits water to penetrate even in the closed position, is not obstructed.

### 4.10. SEA WATER FILTER

If a sea water filter is installed in the water pump intake line, the cover should be transparent in order to permit observation of the flow of the cooling water and any contamination of the filter.

**Attention:** After cleaning of filter it has to be checked that the cover is refitted carefully preventing any air to be aspirated by the water pump.

### 4.11. FUEL FILTER

The life of the fuel filter depends entirely on the degree of purity of the fuel used. A loss of engine power may be due to a shortage of fuel brought about by a clogged filter. If this is suspected the air vent screw in the fuel pump should be opened. Unsteady flow, even after pumping, indicates a contaminated filter. Change the filter element (see fig. 13). We recommend a PUROLATOR PM 456 filter element.

A water contaminated fuel system causes fuel filter paper element to become water-logged which results in fuel starvation (loss of power).

Fig. 13

### 4.12. BLEEDING

Although all FARYMANN marine engines are equipped with the automatic bleeding system (which requires of course that boat yard has installed a fuel return line to the fuel reservoir) it can occur that fuel system has to be bleeded. Don't loosen banjo bolts or other connectors of fuel lines but only vent screw on injection pump. Operate hand primer on fuel feed pump (Fig. 14) until absolutely bubble-free fuel leaks. Retighten vent screw thoroughly.

Fig. 14

## 4.13 MECHANICAL FUEL FEED PUMP

The pump, fitted with a screen in the inlet banjo bolt (14), is equipped in addition with a fuel strainer (2). Both should be checked and possibly cleaned about every 60 hours.

After cleaning outside of pump and dismounting of cover (1) lift out joint (8) and plastic strainer (2). Wash strainer in clean fuel and put it back with pins on strainer turned upwards. After fitting of cover (1) bleed fuel lines.

When refitting banjo bolts always use new copper washers.

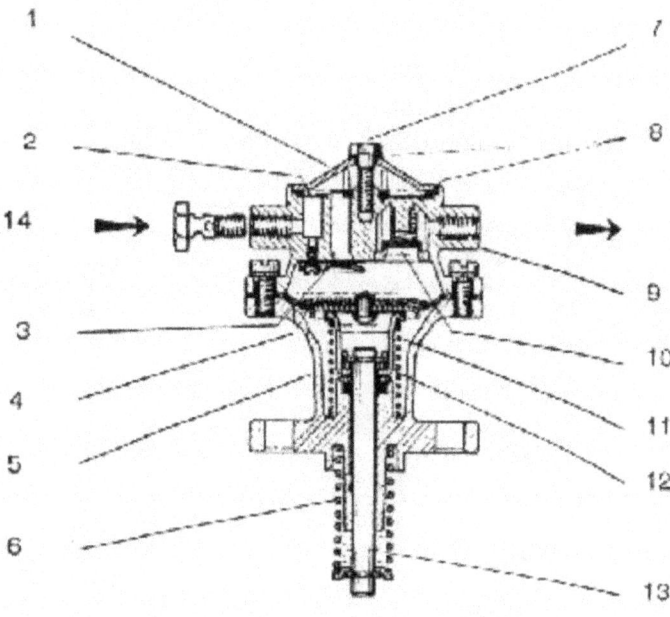

| | | | |
|---|---|---|---|
| 1 | Cover | 8 | Joint |
| 2 | Fuel strainer | 9 | Headcasting |
| 3 | Intake valve | 10 | Exit valve |
| 4 | Diaphragm | 11 | Spring (diaphragm) |
| 5 | Pump body | 12 | Retainer |
| 6 | Spring (plunger) | 13 | Plunger |
| 7 | Screw | 14 | Banjo bolt |

### 4.14 CHANGING THE GEAR OIL

With new gearbox oil has to be changed after max. 25 hours.

If a line for connecting a hand pump is not provided, the gearbox top cover must be opened and the oil removed by means of a hand drain pump.

### 4.15 GREASING THE STARTER RIM GEAR

The starter pinion should mesh well over the entire length of teeth. Remove the starter. Lightly grease the rim gear with the aid of a brush. Use e.g. BOSCH FT 1 V 31 grease.

### 4.16 BATTERY

Add only clean distilled water. Protect terminals with a light vaseline coating.

## 5. STORAGE OF ENGINE

Read this entire section before proceeding with lay-up!

If the engine is to be taken out of service for a lengthy period, e.g. during the winter, protect engine as outlined below:

Frost protection has already been dealt with in Para. 3.3.6.

The diesel engine must be protected from rust, irrespective of whether the boat is laid up on land or the engine removed. Rust e.g. in the fuel injection system can cause engine failure even where its presence cannot be detected with the naked eye.

### 5.1 LUBE-OIL AND FUEL SYSTEM

1) Clean the outside of the engine with diesel fuel or white spirit.

2) Drain off the engine oil while it is still warm and fill with anticorrosive engine oil, e.g. SHELL ENSIS 20 or ESSO RUST BAN up to the lower dipstick mark (MIN.).

3) Drain the fuel tank and clean it thoroughly. Drain the fuel filter. Then fill the fuel tank with several litres of a mixture of diesel fuel and SHELL ENSIS or ESSO RUST BAN at a ratio of 2 : 1. Bleed the fuel system.

4) Allow the engine to run for approx. 15 minutes so that all the pipelines, filters, pump and nozzles are filled with the protective fluid and the anticorrosive engine oil mixture is evenly distributed inside the engine.

5) Remove the rocker arm cover and spray a mixture of diesel fuel and 10% SHELL ENSIS 20 on rocker arms, fit covers again.

6) With the speed lever at full power and the decompression lever actuated, so that engine will not fire, crank the engine several times so that the cylinder is well sprayed with the diesel fuel anti-corrosive mixture. Drain anti-corrosive oil from sump.

7) Remove the exhaust piping from the cylinder head or the exhaust manifold and cover the exhaust ports by means of adhesive tape. This also applies to the port

5.2. **COOLING WATER SYSTEM**

Cooling chambers of cylinders, cylinder heads, and exhaust manifold to be filled up with emulsifying cooling water protective oil, for instance SHELL DONAX C or equal. After 15 minutes, drain oil as detailed in para 3.3.6.

Engine to be externally cleaned, and machined parts to be covered with protective oil (bowden cables, operating levers and joints on engine and in the cockpit not to be forgotten).

5.3. **ELECTRIC SYSTEM**

Battery to be removed and taken to a charging station for maintenance and care.

Finally a sign should be put on the engine, referring to the protective measures taken against corrosion.

6. **RESTORING TO SERVICE**

Although this subject has been dealt with in detail in Para. 1, we shall once again list the most important points.

6.1. Fill the fuel tank, test for unimpeded flow with the fuel filter installed and if necessary change the filter cartridge. Fill crankcase with specified HD lube-oil, take battery on board and connect. Coat terminals with vaseline after tightening.

6.2. Take out fuel injection nozzles, clean and if possible have them immediately tested by your local BOSCH service-station, for correct injection pressure. With injector out, turn the engine starter in order to remove anti-rust oil from cylinder. Re-fit injection nozzles.

6.3. Bleed fuel system, and connect all fuel-, water- and exhaust lines etc. Remember to remove the **plugs**. Check all water and fuel lines for leaks.

6.4. Start engine and make trial run, checking immediately whether the cooling water is flowing through the sea water filter to the engine. Re-check all lines, seals, and hose connections for leaks.

## 7. TROUBLE SHOOTING

**7.1.** Faults are usually due to inadequate maintenance. In the event of a fault, first check whether all the points in these operating instructions have been followed.

If you cannot detect and remedy the fault even with the aid of the following table, it is essential that you apply to the nearest FARYMANN dealer or approved service station.

In order to ensure good service, always state engine type and serial number, e.g. 26 A 30 1026.

**7.2.**

| FAULT | POSSIBLE CAUSE | REMEDY |
|---|---|---|
| Engine does not start | Control lever at STOP | When starting always place at MAX. and if necessary operate excess starting fuel |
| | Fuel tank empty | Top up tank and bleed fuel lines |
| | Fuel filter clogged or waterlogged | Replace filter element |
| | Air in fuel system | Bleed |
| | Starter does not turn freely | Charge battery, examine terminals and tighten. (Emergency: use decompression device) |
| | Engine oil too viscous, espec. at low ambient temperatures | Use HD SAE 10 lube-oil |
| | No compression, valve clearance incorrect | Adjust valve |
| Engine runs erratically, no output | Fuel supply too low, filter clogged | Replace fuel filter element, check contents of tank |
| | Inadequate supply of combustion air | Engine cowling (housing) must have opening for fresh air supply |
| | Air in fuel system | Bleed |
| | Fuel pressure lines leaking | Tighten |
| | Valve clearance incorrect | Adjust valve |
| Engine stalls when warm | Gasoline in fuel (gas bubbles are formed) | Empty fuel tank, filter etc. fill with clean diesel fuel, bleed fuel system. |

7.2.

| FAULT | POSSIBLE CAUSE | REMEDY |
|---|---|---|
| Exhaust emits excessive smoke: 1) blue | Engine oil level too high | Drain off and re-check oil level, possibly check angle of engine |
| | Valve clearance incorrect | Adjust valve clearance |
| | Poor compression due to seized or broken piston rings, worn valve guides etc | Have engine overhauled |
| 2) black | Engine overloaded | Reduce propeller diameter |
| | Excess starting fuel device cannot disengage itself as engine does not reach rated speed (overloaded) | Briefly move speed control lever into idling position, then slowly back to full load |
| Engine runs too hot | Engine compartment too hot | Fresh air must be adequately ventilated |
| | Too little cooling water | Open sea cock completely |
| | | Clean sea water filter |
| | | Clean water inlet strainer (outboard) |
| | **Oil level too high** | **Drain oil; check engine inclination, respective sump capacity and dipstick markings with chart — page 9/10** |
| | Waterpump aspirates air through cover of seawater filter or loose hose clamp | Wing nut not tightened, rubber gasket defective |
| | Cooling water line defective | Check water lines |
| | Pump impeller defective | Fit new impeller |
| | Cooling water pump rotates too slowly | Tighten drive V-belt |
| | Thermostat defective | Clean or replace. In case of doubt continue operation without thermostat. |
| | Injection nozzle defective | Have nozzle checked by mechan. |
| | Feed rate of injection pump erratic | Examine by mechanic |

7.2

| FAULT | POSSIBLE CAUSE | REMEDY |
|---|---|---|
| Engine runs too hot | Engine cooling passages scaled up or clogged with sludge | Dismantle and clean engine (service station) |
| Oil pressure pilot lamp lights up | Pressure switch defective | Fit a new switch |
| | Oil pressure too low | Stop engine immediately. Check oil level |
| | Oil level too low | Top up |
| | Oil level too high | Crankshaft action creates oil foam which enters lube oil pump causing pressure failure. Correct oil level. |
| | Oil filter leaky | Tighten or replace filter |
| | Oil filter clogged | Replace oil filter immediately |
| | Worn bearings | See service station |
| Engine races | Centrifugal governor defective | Do not disengage propeller, return with lowest possible speed, apply to service station |
| Engine knocks | Worn connecting rod bearings | See service station |
| | Valve sticks | Check valves (lubrication, clearances) |
| | Fuel delivery timing incorrect, piston tends to seize up | Stop engine, let it cool, turn crank, in case of difficulty have boat towed |
| Charge indicator lamp lights up during operation | Alternator speed too low | Tighten V-belt |
| | Terminals loose | Tighten terminals and cable ends |
| | Voltage regulator defective | Take to repair |
| Engine does not obtain its stated speed under load | Engine overloaded | Reduce propeller diameter |

## FUEL SYSTEM

Fuel system with automatic bleeding device, enrproving fuel feed pump (2). Same continuously passes fuel through filter (4) to fuel injection pump (5). Part of the excessive fuel returns via banjo bolt with built-in throttle (8) and fuel return line (10) to fuel tank.

The return line connecting to tank should be situated as low as possible (5 cm above bottom), to prevent air penetrating fuel system via return line (10) when the engine does not run.

Drain plug (9) for drainage of condensing water and deposits in the tank, if any.

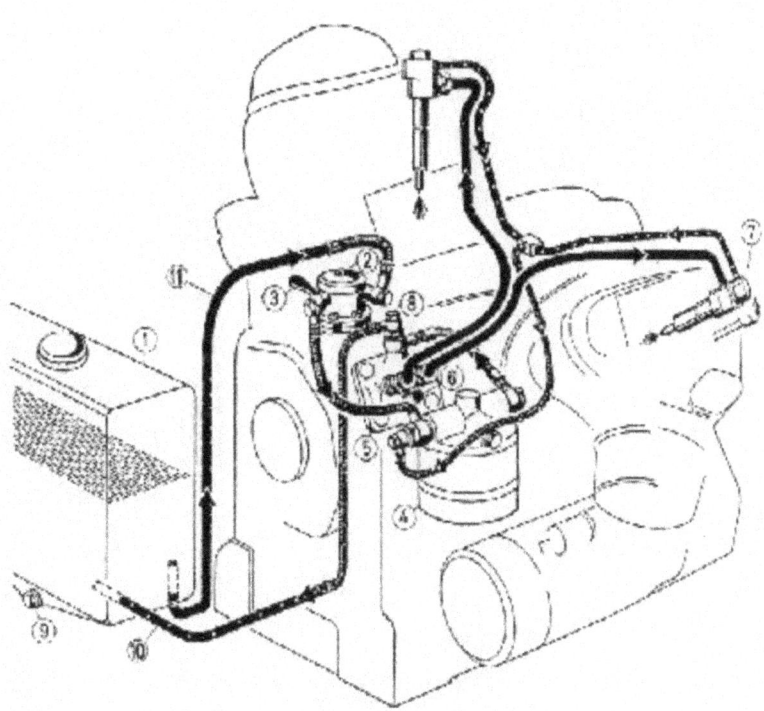

1. Fuel tank
2. Fuel feed pump (with pre.-filter)
3. Primer (fuel feed pump)
4. Fuel filter
5. Injection pump
6. Push button for excess starting fuel
7. Injection nozzle
8. Banjo bolt with throttle
9. Drain plug
10. Fuel return line
11. Fuel feed line

## FARYMANN MARINE DIESEL ENGINE

Exhaust and cooling water installation diagram.
Direct seawater cooling with water injection into exhaust **above water line**.

A = 100 mm (4")

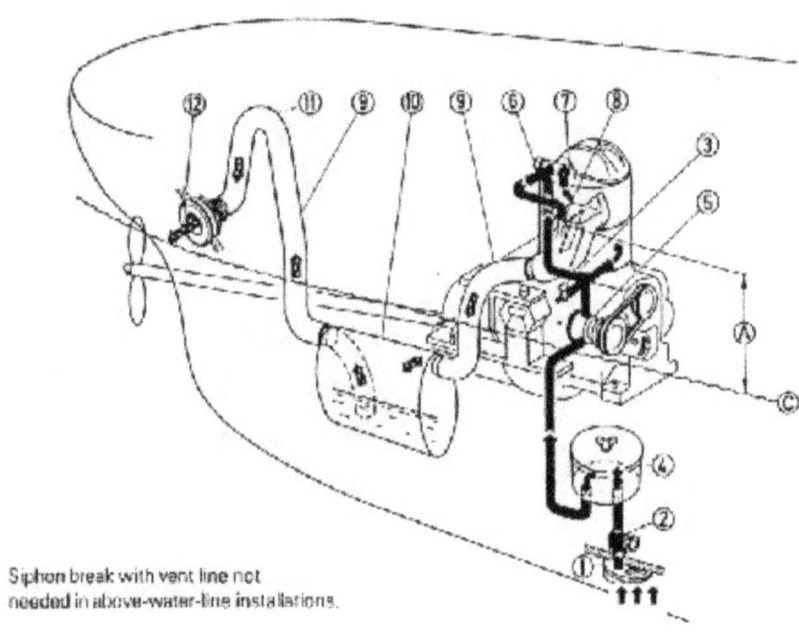

Siphon break with vent line not
needed in above-water-line installations.

C = Water line
A = Minimum height above water line of water injection into exhaust line.

| | | | |
|---|---|---|---|
| 1 | Seawater strainer | 7 | Thermostat |
| 2 | Sea cock | 8 | Water injection |
| 3 | Drain cock | 9 | Rubber hose |
| 4 | Seawater filter | 10 | Water lift silencer |
| 5 | Water pump | 11 | Goose neck |
| 6 | Temp. Connector | 12 | Exhaust outlet (thru hull fitting) |

# FARYMANN MARINE DIESEL ENGINE

Exhaust and cooling water installation
Direct seawater cooling with water injection into exhaust below water line

A = 300 mm (12")
B = 100 mm (4")

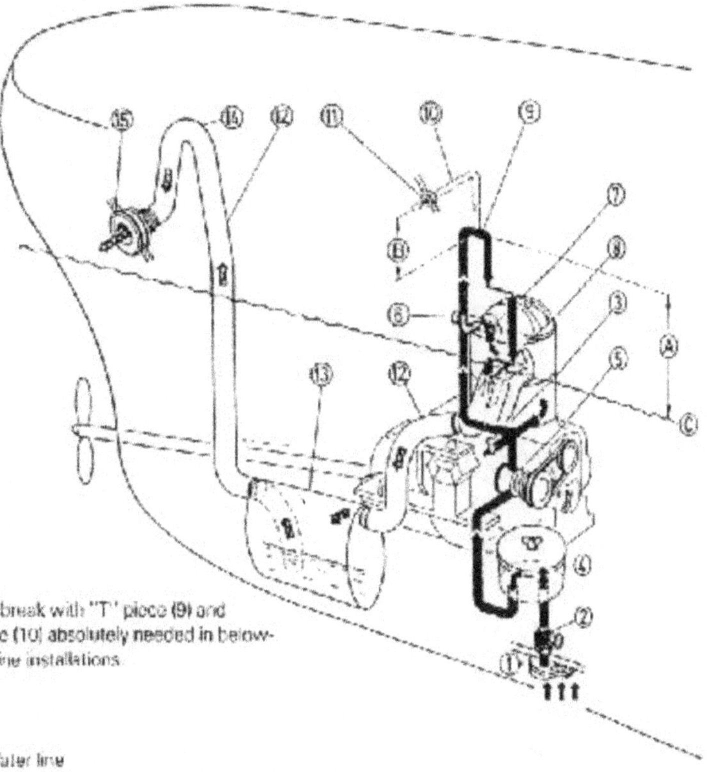

Siphon break with "T" piece (9) and vent line (10) absolutely needed in below-water-line installations.

C = Water line
A = Minimum height above water line of water injection into exhaust line.

| | | | | | |
|---|---|---|---|---|---|
| 1 | Seawater strainer | 7 | Thermostat | 12 | Rubber hose |
| 2 | Sea cock | 8 | Water injection | 13 | Waterlift silencer |
| 3 | Drain cock | 9 | Water line with T-fitting | 14 | Goose neck |
| 4 | Seawater filter | | | 15 | Hull fitting (exhaust) |
| 5 | Water pump | 10 | Breather line | | |
| 6 | Temp. Connector | 11 | Hull fitting | | |

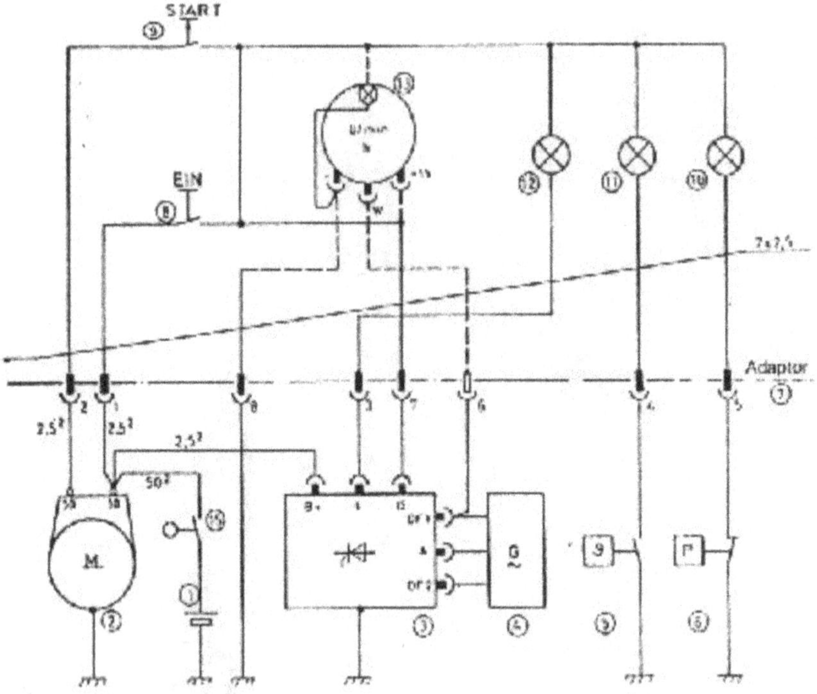

## WIRING DIAGRAM K 34 M

1. Battery
2. Starter Motor
3. Governor
4. Generator
5. Temp. switch
6. Oil pressure switch
7. Adapter
8. Operating button
9. Starter button
10. Pilot lamp (lube oil pressure)
11. Temp. pilot lamp
12. Pilot lamp (battery charge)
13. Tachometer
15. Battery main switch | Spec. ordering

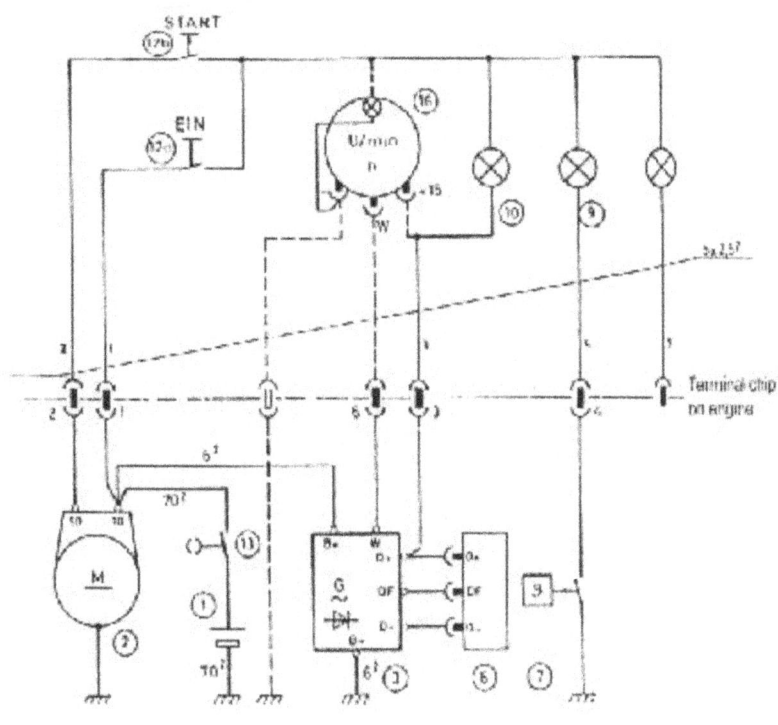

## WIRING DIAGRAM L 30 M

| | | | |
|---|---|---|---|
| 1 | Battery | 10 | Pilot lamp (battery charge) |
| 2 | Starter Motor | 12a | Operating switch |
| 3 | Generator | 12b | Starter switch |
| 6 | Governor | 13 | Battery main switch |
| 7 | Temp. switch | 16 | Tachometer |
| 9 | Temp. pilot lamp | | |

Spec. ordering

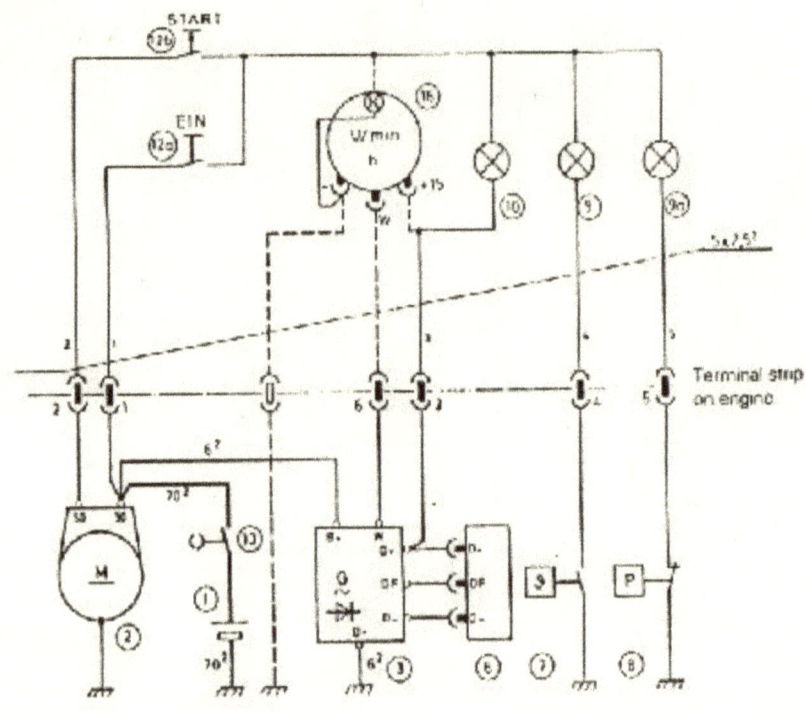

**WIRING DIAGRAM R 30 M, S 30 M**

| | | | | |
|---|---|---|---|---|
| 1 | Battery | 9a | Pilot lamp (lube oil pressure) | |
| 2 | Starter | 10 | Pilot lamp (battery charge) | |
| 3 | Generator | 12a | Operating button | |
| 6 | Governor | 12b | Starter switch | |
| 7 | Temp. switch | 13 | Battery main switch | Spec. ordering |
| 8 | Oil pressure switch | 16 | Tachometer | |
| 9 | Temp. pilot lamp | | | |

## SINGLE LEVER REMOTE CONTROL

1. Speed regulating cable in idling position
2. Gear control cable in neutral position
3. Stop cable with stop button

Control gear

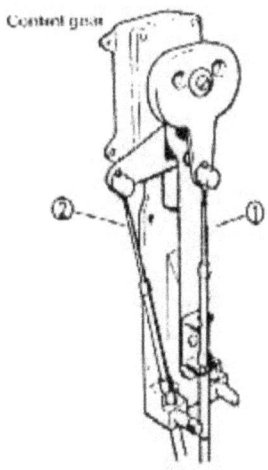

## ADJUSTMENT:

Bring control gear and engine speed regulation in position as shown.

1) Length of speed control cable (1) to be adjusted, so that speed regulating lever (4) rests against stop for idling (6).

2) Adjust additional stroke „s" of stop cable (3) to at least the length necessary to move engine speed regulating lever (5) up to full load stop (7) without any obstruction.

3) Adjust gear control lever (8) in slotted hole until feed path of control gear is the same as that of the reversing reduction gear.

Regulation

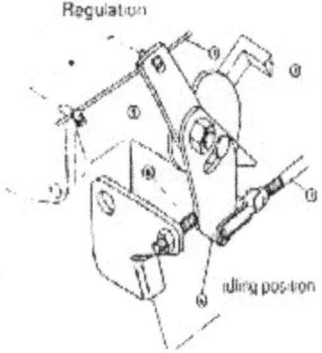

idling position

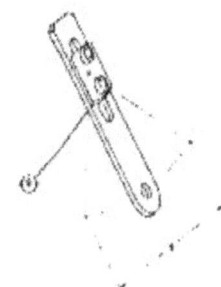

www.ingramcontent.com/pod-product-compliance
Lightning Source LLC
Chambersburg PA
CBHW031127160426
43192CB00008B/1146